I Do

125 YEARS OF WEDDINGS IN NEW ZEALAND

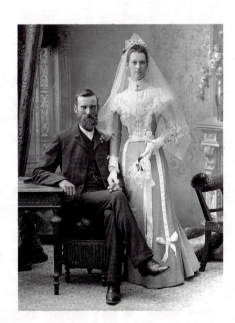

Sandra Coney

HODDER MOA BECKETT

To & All the Family with love from David & Margaret (see P.55)

The publisher and author wish to thank all the people and organisations who have contributed photographs and provided information for this book. They have made every effort to trace owners of copyright material, acknowledge sources and confirm facts contained in *I Do – 125 Years of Weddings in New Zealand*. Should any errors or omissions have occurred, they would like to offer their apologies. On receiving advice, appropriate acknowledgements and information will be included in further editions.

ISBN 1-86958-171-7

© 1995 Sandra Coney

Published in 1995 by Hodder Moa Beckett Publishers Limited
(a member of the Hodder Headline group)
28 Poland Road, Glenfield, Auckland, New Zealand

Designed by Sally Hollis-McLeod
Printed through Colorcraft, Hong Kong
Cover design by Trevor Newman

All rights reserved. No part of this publication may be reproduced or transmitted in any form by any means, electronic or mechanical, including photocopying, recording, or any information storage and retrieval system, without permission in writing from the publisher.

Contents

Introduction 4

The Wedding – An Enduring Tradition 6

1
Visions in White 14
WEDDINGS IN THE VICTORIAN ERA

2
The Grand Occasion 28
WEDDINGS IN THE EDWARDIAN ERA

Marvels of the Confectioners' Art 38
WEDDING CAKES

3
Plain Elegance 40
THE FIRST WORLD WAR PERIOD

Little Charmers 46
BRIDESMAIDS AND FLOWER GIRLS

4
The Flapper Brides 48
WEDDINGS IN THE 1920s

5
The Glamour Weddings 56
HOLLYWOOD INFLUENCES THE 1930s

6
Hasty Marriages and Fabric Shortages 66
WEDDINGS IN THE SECOND WORLD WAR PERIOD

The Nuptial Bounty 74
WEDDING PRESENTS

7
Conservative Years 76
LITTLE CHANGE IN THE 1950s

An Abundance of Flowers 82
BRIDAL BOUQUETS OVER THE YEARS

8
Changing Traditions 86
WEDDINGS IN THE 1960s AND 1970s

9
The New Romantics 92
THE REVIVAL OF THE WHITE WEDDING

Introduction

BEFORE COMPILING THIS BOOK my own experience of weddings was somewhat limited. For generations no one in the direct line of my family has had a traditional white wedding. A desire for privacy and Scottish practicality dictated something more simple: my mother even removed the corsage from her green wedding suit before she and my father visited a studio photographer so he would not know the two had just married. Members of the wider family did have more formal weddings. The several Battersby photographs in this book come from my father's mother's side. My father features as best man to his brother, Bryan Pearce, and my mother as bridesmaid to her sister, Irene Hellen Morgan.

I first delved into the subject of weddings when working on the Suffrage Year project, *Standing in the Sunshine*. However, when I researched the subject for that book *and* then again for this project I was surprised at how little attention had been given to the subject of weddings, especially in Western nations.

In the past history has tended to focus on the public world of men – on politics, employment, war and major national events. The private world of women – the world of relationships, the home, child-rearing, housework and voluntary work – has received far less attention. These were deemed to be the province of the sociologist, the psychologist or anthropologist rather than the historian or museum curator.

Social science researchers have tended to look beyond their own shores for interesting subject matter, ignoring what was under their noses. Wedding rituals in Northern India or Africa have had more attention than those closer to home. And yet the wedding is the principal social ritual of Western societies and its star shows no signs of dimming.

More recently, there has been a growing recognition that the private world is worthy of study. Rituals such as weddings or funerals and subjects such as costume are at last starting to be studied and written about.

Some parameters were set for this book and some guidelines were followed in choosing photographs. Firstly, this is a book about weddings, rather than marriage. It tracks wedding fashions, customs and rituals – the way they have changed and the way they have stayed intact.

The scope of the book has to some extent been limited by the existence and availability of images. For instance, there are no photographs of wedding showers or stag nights. If these exist, they have not entered the public collections (or any private ones I looked at). Weddings are to a large degree an occasion on which romance, celebration and beauty rule. There can undoubtedly be

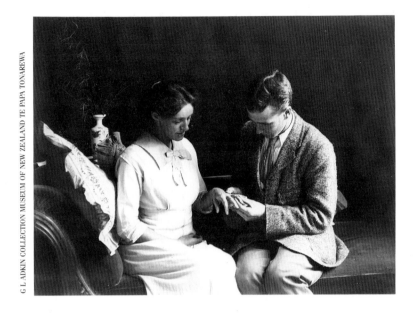

Photographer George Leslie Adkin re-enacted the moment of his proposal to Maud Herd.

tensions, traumas and misery at weddings, but these occur in the background, off the record. At weddings families record what they want to record. In contrast to documentary photography, the couple are the clients and they determine how this event will be represented to the world. This leads to a certain formality. People are prepared. They have had time to set their faces and arrange their clothes. Yet this controlled process is also a strength. There are few other times in people's lives when they deliberately present themselves as they want to be seen for posterity.

The choice of the photographs in *I Do* was not dictated by what was quirky or different, but rather by how a particular photograph typified a practice, costume or change in style. Photographs had to be good examples of a custom and show detail to be included in the book.

I hope *I Do* will be an enjoyable book for people to look at and read, but it will also be a useful resource for anyone studying changing costume styles, as well as genealogists and family history researchers wanting guidance in dating photographs. Wherever possible the photographs have been accurately dated from families, marriage indexes or registers. Those planning weddings may also find inspiration in the weddings of the past.

The Wedding
AN ENDURING TRADITION

THE WEDDING IS THE LAST GREAT RITE of passage of contemporary Western societies. An individual's journey through life was once punctuated by events and ceremonies marking transitions on the journey from childhood to maturity. More liberal sexual mores, tolerance of different living styles, greater secularism, looser family ties, the economic independence of the young, and the changed role of women have combined to make many former rites of passage less relevant. Rituals such as 'coming out' (the entry of a girl into womanhood), and formal mourning are not practised at all, while others such as christenings, being presented, 21st birthdays, and engagements are observed less frequently and usually in a much more low-key way. Only the wedding has retained its status as a rite of passage. Its persistence can be put down to a communally felt need to resist the final loss of these community rituals. Weddings provide social cohesion: they look both forward and backward. They symbolise the creation of a new family unit and faith in the future as well as stability, conservatism and tradition.

Weddings are celebrated less often in the late twentieth century. In New Zealand in 1994 they reached a 30-year low. An increase in the number of informal de facto unions and a tendency to marry late have led to fewer marriages.

But although there may be fewer weddings, and the reasons for marrying may be changing, weddings are celebrated with no less vigour and enthusiasm than they ever have been. In the 1990s, many families put a huge effort into weddings. A survey by *Bride and Groom* magazine in 1992 showed that the average expenditure on a wedding was nearly $15,000, while some families spent as much as $88,000.

Weddings have been a cause for celebration for centuries. Some elements of the wedding rituals can be traced back to Roman or pagan practices, but the wedding in the form that is now commonly regarded as 'traditional' is a relatively recent creation.

In the first half of the nineteenth century, the wedding tended to be a low-key affair. For early settlers, arriving in New Zealand from Europe, marriage was largely a practical and economic arrangement, although attraction would have played some part in many decisions to wed. Writing on the European family in New Zealand, the historians Erik Olssen and Andree Levesque explain that 'Virtually nobody in the early or mid-Victorian period would have considered sexual compatibility or personal fulfilment as reasons for marriage. . .' Women looked for security in the form of a good worker, and men sought the advantage of a proficient 'helpmeet' to organise the home. Marriage was primarily an economic partnership.

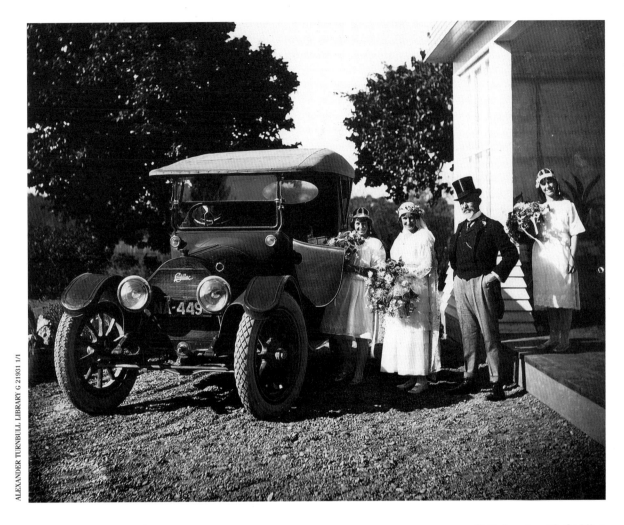

Bridal party with Cadillac.

Weddings at the time were quite plain affairs. The bride and groom wore their best clothes and holidays such as Christmas Day and New Year's Day were popular wedding dates as they allowed friends to gather and celebrate.

The white wedding was inspired by a series of weddings by members of the British royal family during the mid-nineteenth century. The weddings of the children of Queen Victoria in the 1860s defined how society folk and the newly emerging middle class should celebrate weddings. These were dreamy, romantic affairs with the brides in a froth of white tulle and lace, accompanied by a bevy of pretty bridesmaids.

The white wedding was speedily adopted by Maori for whom the rituals and pageant proved attractive. In the

1860s Lady Barker described a Maori bride in 'white muslin costume, ornamented with white satin bows'. The impact of Christianity also meant that church weddings were desirable.

Traditional Maori wedding rituals varied according to the status of the participants. Different forms are described by Makareti in her book, *The Old-Time Maori*. Marriages were usually an alliance between hapu or iwi and were often arranged. Alliances between rangatira (chiefly) people involved grand ceremonials with days of feasting, speeches and entertainment. Among ordinary people of the hapu, there was very little ceremonial: the respective parents were consulted and if there was no objection the man and woman simply slept together.

Successive laws required Maori to conform to Pakeha requirements with a formal ceremony conducted by an authorised person, and a marriage certificate. The Maori Purposes Act of 1951 finally abolished any recognition of Maori marriage forms, although it was still not uncommon for the families of intending couples to meet to agree to the union as late as the 1950s and 1960s.

The development of the wedding as the major social ritual of Pakeha society occurred between 1880 and 1900 and denoted the more settled nature of New Zealand society. The white wedding emerged as a display of social standing and economic status. Gradually it filtered through all social strata, symbolising the aspirations of artisans, tradespeople and working families to improve their position in the world.

While the form of the ritual emulated British practices, the wedding had additional meanings in colonial society. Many immigrants had left behind their extended family: a significant number had emigrated as single men and women. Alliances through marriage encouraged the development of wider social groupings and support systems and weddings reinforced these new social and familial networks by formally bringing people together. In hard-working colonial society the wedding also provided an opportunity for socialising and for fun, as well as a place to meet members of the opposite sex.

The elaboration of the wedding rituals reflected the significance accorded to the couple's transition from the single to the married state. The family and home were invested with particular sentimentality during the latter years of Victoria's reign and the early part of the twentieth century. The home was the bulwark of society and the wife in particular had the role of creating and building the home. The mother was the guardian not only of her own family's, but society's moral purity, Godliness and order. The wedding was sanctified as the entry of the woman into this socially important role. The church wedding gained in popularity, supplanting the more informal wedding in the home. While couples by and large continued to marry within their class and continued to consider the practical and economic assets of their partners, marriages were increasingly love matches and were undertaken as a personal choice. Companionship and fulfilment were sought from marriage partners, and sexual attraction grew in importance. This was reflected in the number of weddings which were precipitated by pregnancy. By 1913, more than one-third of brides under 30 were pregnant on their wedding day.

Marrying for love gradually overtook all other considerations as the principle reason for marrying. As the number of children born to a family decreased dramatically in the twentieth century – the average number of births to a married woman was 4.7 in 1891, but 2.4 in 1923 – the importance of emotional and sexual relationships increased. The increasing freedom of young women and the influence of the cinema, with its preoccupation with courtship and romance, encouraged this change in emphasis.

A guard of honour of tennis rackets at the wedding of Mr and Mrs MacKenzie, about 1930.

The high status accorded to weddings was accompanied by the development of a variety of support services. Originally families planned and carried out weddings. Studio photographers, hired to express the ritual intentions of the wedding drama, were the first paid professionals to play a part in weddings. Gradually more and more aspects of the wedding were professionalised, aiding the development of a wedding industry involving photographers, dress-makers, florists, confectioners, providers of transport and caterers. From the late nineteenth century, the social pages of newspapers and magazines reported on weddings and even published photographs of high society matches.

Throughout the twentieth century, weddings of the British royal family continued to set the style and tone of weddings. The weddings of Princess Mary, eldest daughter of George V, in 1922, and of Lady Elizabeth Bowes-Lyon (Queen Mother) to the Duke of York in 1923 delivered the British Empire from the practical plainness of wartime weddings. Both brides wore exquisitely embroidered tunic-style dresses and were accompanied by eight bridesmaids.

The Duke and Duchess of York's wedding in 1934 was the first royal wedding ceremony to be filmed, allowing people all around the world to view the event at the cinema on news reels. Princess Marina has been described as 'the first royal bride to assume the role of fashion icon'. A glamorous, stylish woman, Marina wore figure-hugging silver brocade in a medieval style and a diamond tiara. 'Princess Marina' brides appeared all around the Commonwealth, substituting paste and cut glass for the real thing.

The wedding of Princess Elizabeth at Westminster Abbey in 1947 had a similar effect to that of the previous generation of royal weddings in banishing wartime austerity. Brides during the Second World War had been hindered by food and fabric shortages, as well as the belief that extravagance was inappropriate when nations were in peril and men were going off to die. Princess Elizabeth's dress contained 10,000 pearls and there were 12 official wedding cakes. The main cake weighed 900

10 THE WEDDING

Cutting the cake at the Kyle-Robinson wedding.

pounds and was nine feet high. The future Queen's wedding was seen as embodying family values as well as strengthening the British Commonwealth as a family of nations.

The post-War period was one of quiet home and family life and this conservatism was reflected in weddings. There was little adventurousness in the way weddings were celebrated. Various rituals were carefully observed, more from superstition than anything else, as their real meaning had been lost long ago. The silver cardboard shoe carried by many brides in the 1950s and 1960s, and the practice of tying shoes to the honeymoon car, go back to the Middle Ages when the father of the bride took a shoe from the bride and gave it to the groom, who tapped the bride's head with it to denote the change in ownership. Confetti was a substitute for the wheat, rice or fruit thrown in Roman times to ensure fecundity. At weddings in the post-War years these practices had simply come to denote good luck.

Major challenges to the wedding ceremonials began to occur in the late 1960s and intensified in the 1970s. At the same time as New Zealand experienced higher than ever marriage rates, and the lowest average ages of brides and grooms ever recorded (21.19 for brides and 23.6 for grooms in 1971), wedding practices began to modify. The new teen-based popular culture demanded a new style of weddings which reflected the mores and icons of the young. Bridal parties in the seventies could be startling. Ministers reeled as brides in lime-green gowns and grooms in caftans came down the aisle. Informality and casualness were sought by many couples, and there was often an uneasy truce between parents with their expectations of a traditional wedding and their offsprings' desire to 'do something different'.

The 'sexual revolution' of the sixties threatened the value of the 'virgin' bride in her symbolically white robe. A large number of brides were confined within the first seven months of marriage (6437 in 1971 compared with 4625 in 1962). In such circumstances it was not considered proper to marry in white, although many did, but there was an increasing sense that many of those who were not pregnant were only lucky, or were simply wiser in the ways of the world. Tradition was less valued by this generation, who saw much of it as hypocrisy and pretence.

The other challenge to traditional practices came from the women's liberation movement. It denounced traditional marriage and its trappings as oppressive to women and criticised the wedding ceremonials as a transfer of ownership in which the woman passed from one male owner – her father – to another – her husband. The bride's ring was a remnant of the 'bride price' and symbolised ownership.

Enjoying the entertainment at their wedding: Richelle Kahui and Kelly McConnell (centre), 1993.

Increasingly, couples didn't marry at all. As social disapproval of de facto unions dwindled, this option was taken up by growing numbers of couples. Between 1981 and 1991 the proportion of New Zealanders (over the age of 15) living with de facto partners increased from 3.8 to 6.2 per cent. Eleven per cent of couples living together in 1991 were in de facto relationships. This increase has coincided with a fall in the proportion of people married, from the peak of 45.3 marriages per 1000 not-married people in 1971 to 18.8 per 1000 in 1994. The importance of work and careers for women has contributed to later marriages, part of a worldwide trend. The average age for first-time brides was 26.6 in 1994, 28.6 for first-time grooms; ages more similar to those of the late nineteenth century than those of the immediate post-War years. Only one in 31 marriages in 1994 were to teenage women while in 1971 one in three marriages were to teenage women. Remarriage has also increased more than two-fold in the last quarter century. In 1994 one in three marriages involved the remarriage of one or both partners.

In the 1980s and 1990s there has been a revival in traditional weddings. The catalyst for this was the wedding of Lady Diana Spencer to the Prince of Wales in 1981. The Princess of Wales set the style for romantic, fairy-tale weddings. People throughout the world were regaled with details of the event. The wedding as dramatic theatre became popular again.

Princess Diana was the traditional virgin bride who on marriage subsumed herself in the role of consort to her husband. This is not the role of most modern brides. They

The bride in ivory satin and five bridesmaids in cream cashmere laced with gold cord at the wedding of Dr James Hudson to Beatrix Andrew at the All Saints Church, Nelson, in 1886.

are usually earners in their own right who will expect to continue to earn, even if they have time out of the paid workforce to have children. So what is the attraction of the Princess Diana-style wedding?

In an essay on weddings, feminist author Naomi Wolf argued that 'there is a terrible spiritual longing among women for social behaviour or ritual that respects, even worships, female sexuality and reproductive potential'.

Although surrounded by media images of glamour and sophistication, most women lack these in their actual lives. The wedding provides an opportunity for a woman to be admired simply as a woman and to represent herself in the starring role In a romantic drama of her own creation. As it is only for a day, there is no danger that the role of princess will be permanent.

In recent decades the patriarchal meaning of many of the marriage rituals has diminished along with the religious content. Couples not infrequently design their own wedding ceremonies, sometimes with the help of a lay marriage celebrant. Where couples have previously been married, their children may be involved in the ceremony, and sons or daughters have been known to give their mothers away. Weddings are held outdoors, in homes, or at the reception venue, and some adventurous couples have gone to great lengths to find their own unique location.

The influx of new immigrants after the Second World War has led to a greater variety in wedding practices, although some cultural groups, such as the Chinese and Pacific Islands peoples, adopted the European Christian ceremony in part or entirely.

Even in more traditional weddings some practices have changed, others have been abandoned. Brides in the 1990s may wear white, but it has entirely lost its symbolic meaning of sexual innocence. Brides no longer pretend to be virginal. The bride of the 1990s may choose to look sensual, even sexy, her costume revealing a great deal of bosom and skin. Her aim is to be admired.

Brides rarely promise to 'obey', and the wedding breakfast speeches, traditionally reserved for the men of the party, may now be shared with the bride or bridesmaids. Brides are given away by a variety of people or not at all. Rings, once worn only by brides, are now often exchanged between husband and wife.

The pressure on young people to marry and have a traditional wedding has considerably diminished in the past two decades, although it still exists in some families. For most people, the decision to enter marriage and celebrate this at a wedding is now an active choice. Previously people married for a variety of reasons in addition to love: for security, for sex, because of social pressure, or because the woman was pregnant. In the 1990s these reasons are less important, yet, although many couples have been living together before they marry, may even have children, the wedding has not diminished in emotional meaning. The wedding is still regarded as a public proclamation of commitment.

Social scientists researching weddings have commented on the symbolic importance many modern couples give to 'following tradition'. Although the religious content of weddings has diminished, many believe a traditional wedding will imbue the ceremony with seriousness and significance. Gathering relatives as witnesses is seen as important in affirming the new couple's place in a wider family network.

Weddings are rich cultural dramas in which participants play out almost tribal beliefs about the way they want society to be ordered. They embed the couple in their familial and social surroundings. For women, weddings are the last great female ritual, an opportunity to be unashamedly centre-stage. As we near the end of the twentieth century, there is little sign that weddings are in any danger of vanishing.

CHAPTER ONE

Visions in White

WEDDINGS IN THE VICTORIAN ERA

THE TRADITION OF WHITE WEDDINGS dates back to the mid-nineteenth century. It followed the fashionable style set by members of the British royal family. At her wedding in 1862, Queen Victoria's daughter, Princess Alice, wore a simple white frock over a crinoline and was accompanied by a bevy of similarly dressed bridesmaids. This early photograph of a society wedding from Nelson shows how quickly this style was copied in the colonies by those who could afford it. Maria Georgiana Monro, daughter of the Speaker of the House of Representatives, married the geologist and explorer James Hector in 1868. The bride wears a simple frock with a crinoline petticoat. The groom wears light-coloured trousers and a frock coat, which could have been blue, claret or mulberry, and carries a top hat, which also could have been a colour such as blue. Colour predominated in fashionable wedding dress for men until the 1890s.

VISIONS IN WHITE 15

FLETCHER COLLECTION, NELSON PROVINCIAL MUSEUM

≫— FEW WEDDING PHOTOGRAPHS WERE TAKEN in the early years of photography. For most early settlers, marriage was a practical, primarily economic arrangement and it was celebrated simply. This photograph of an unidentified couple from Nelson is one of the earliest in the New Zealand collections. The bride wears a plain coloured frock which will continue to be her 'best dress' for some years to come. Her centre-parted hairstyle with a net snood, and the dress's slightly dropped shoulder-line, full sleeves, high neck and crinoline skirt suggest the photograph was taken about 1860. While the bride is the epitome of tidiness, the photographer has neglected to straighten the bridegroom's lapel.

16 VISIONS IN WHITE

⇥ INFLUENCED BY THE MISSIONARIES, many Maori adopted the white Christian wedding from an early date, although informal customary marriage was still practised into the mid-twentieth century. This youthful couple was married at the 'Old Church, Wairoa'. The style of the bride's dress and that of the woman beside her indicate the photo was taken in the 1870s.

⇥ SKIRTS WERE LOADED WITH DECORATION during the late 1870s. The advent of the sewing machine allowed the construction of elaborate ruffles, pleats and ruching. This unidentified Auckland bride wears a divided apron overskirt, which at the back forms a waterfall bustle and train. The sleeves feature ruching, lace frills and buttons, and the long, tight cuirasse bodice is pin-tucked and has rows of lace. The whiteness of the kerchief she holds suggests that the dress was not white. Lilac, cream and pale yellow were popular choices for wedding dresses at this time.

TYREE STUDIO COLLECTION, NELSON PROVINCIAL MUSEUM

BESSIE POYNTER WORE WHITE when she married Arthur John Percival at All Saints Church in Nelson in 1885, but her bridesmaids wear a dark colour, and the three oldest are dressed in unmatching frocks with similar lace collars and Rubens hats. The younger bridesmaids wear matching dresses with box-pleated and draped skirts. The fashion for non-white outfits for bridesmaids was popularised in the 1870s and 1880s. Weddings during this period could be very colourful.

18 VISIONS IN WHITE

TYREE STUDIO COLLECTION, NELSON PROVINCIAL MUSEUM

THE BRIDAL GROUP FROM THE Noakes-Lightband wedding shows how the photographer at the Tyree Studio in Nelson set up the bridal studio, with the skylight in the roof providing light. Daisies, probably real, have been used lavishly on the bridesmaids' flower-pot hats and sprays. The groom, Walter Maplesden Noakes of Kent, sports a single daisy on the lapel of his high-buttoned morning jacket. Jessie Lightband's silk satin frock is trimmed with ruffles of fine lace, as are the bridesmaids' dresses. All have long, very tight-fitting white gloves. The bride's dress is probably a rich creamy silk satin. Most wedding dresses were made of silk and silk was rarely dead white. Marriages were increasingly entered into for romantic reasons as the century went on. The development of the wedding as a romantic ritual reflected this change in the nature of marriage.

THE SAME WEDDING PARTY AS on the previous page photographed with relatives on the tennis court at the bride's parents' home, Wainui House, in Nile Street, Nelson. Tennis was apparently played as tennis rackets can be seen on the ground. In this informal portrait, washing dries on the verandah and two maids with white aprons stand at the rear of the party. A trap waits for the bride and groom at right. The couple married at Christ Church Cathedral in 1885.

TREE STUDIO COLLECTION, NELSON PROVINCIAL MUSEUM

THE FOUR ADULT BRIDESMAIDS OF Edith Boor, daughter of the Superintendent of Nelson Hospital, were virtually indistinguishable from the bride when she married Herbert Burnett, a solicitor, in August 1888. The bodice of the bride's dress is tightly laced in the front and the fabric is probably silk satin. The tightness of the cuirasse bodices and sleeves is seen in the straining of the fabric on the bridesmaids at the back. The bridesmaids' skirts are box pleated in the front, and bunched at the back, while the bride wears an apron overskirt and box-pleated underskirt. The paper or lace ruff used in Victorian posies is well displayed by the bridesmaid on the left.

⇌ LESS WELL-OFF NINETEENTH-CENTURY BRIDES opted for a coloured dress which could be worn for best for some years. Christina Nuttall's dress is decorated only by a frill on the cross-over bodice and a deep row of appliqué around the skirt. The large 'two-yard-square' veil and orange-blossom in her hair are the only features she shares with Edith Boor. Christina's posy was probably professionally made, but the posies carried by other members of the wedding party appear to have been picked from the garden. The groom, Henry Bethwaite, wears a high-lapelled jacket, a waistcoat edged with piping and striped trousers. An outfit such as this might have been bought especially for the wedding, but, carefully looked after, could have lasted for life. The couple married in Nelson in 1891.

TYREE STUDIO COLLECTION, NELSON PROVINCIAL MUSEUM

MARIA NEWMAN HAS BROKEN WITH all photographic tradition by holding her husband Alexander Palmer Herd's hand, even though he seems to be pretending it is not happening. Couples in studio bridal photographs stared solemnly at the camera without physical or visual contact until after the Second World War when styles began to relax. Bride and groom seldom smiled. In the early years this reflected the requirement that photographic subjects remain still and that photographic portraits were valued as a record as much as a sentimental memento. The perseverance of the custom also indicated the solemnity surrounding marriage. The seated bridegroom with standing bride was another custom which persisted, perhaps so that the bride's dress could be fully displayed. Maria's frock is white or cream with another colour. The plain skirt is typical of the 1890s; the only adornment is ribbons tied in true-love knots. The decorative focus of the costume has moved up to the bodice which carries a froth of tulle, lace and pleating. This dress would have carried Maria through many later social events. The couple married at Marlborough in 1898.

TYREE STUDIO COLLECTION, NELSON PROVINCIAL MUSEUM

THE HYDE WEDDING PROVIDES A perfect example of the late Victorian wedding. The women are all sweetness and doe-eyes. Beside them, the balding groom appears a trifle insignificant. A very covered-up look was mandatory in the 1890s. All the women's costumes have high necks and a false jacket front over a pouched plastron. The wide revers spreading over leg o'mutton sleeves were another fashionable feature. The practice of attaching sprigs of orange blossom to the bridal dress started with weddings of the British royal family. The flawless complexions of the bridal party are a credit to the photographer's retoucher. Other photographs of this party show that the women were liberally sprinkled with freckles.

⇛ THE REFORM DRESS WEDDING WAS a protest at the restrictions of Victorian dress. The bride and groom – Kate Walker and James Wilkinson – had written a pamphlet on the subject of dress reform in 1893, likening tight corsets and huge heavy skirts to the Chinese practice of foot binding. They advocated trousers or what they called the 'bifurcated' or 'two-legged' garment. Kate chose blue knickerbockers for her wedding, coupled with a long, cream, gold-embroidered vest and coat. She did not entirely abandon conventional bridal dress, as she is wearing a veil with jasmine. The costume was designed by Alice Burn, seated on the front right, a prominent dress reformer who was told by the Board of Governors not to wear knickerbockers to her lectures at Canterbury University. The wedding was held at Alice's Christchurch home in January 1894 and the photograph of the wedding was widely published, along with derogatory cartoons.

↦ INFORMAL WEDDING PHOTOGRAPHS BEGAN TO appear at the end of the century as new photographic technology made a documentary approach feasible. A large crowd gathered to see the newly wed Mr and Mrs Beard emerge from the church at this Wanganui wedding. By this period, couples often chose a church wedding. Previously nuptials frequently took place in the bride's parents' home, or that of a friend.

F N JONES COLLECTION, ALEXANDER TURNBULL LIBRARY G11445 1/1

TRADITIONALLY BRIDAL PARTIES WENT TO church on foot, but in society weddings the bride often arrived at the church in a horse-drawn carriage, with the driver suitably clad in morning coat and a top hat. The horses wore rosettes and the coachman usually also wore a white rosette and decorated his whip with a ribbon, as can be seen resting on the driver's shoulder in this photograph. When cars took over from coaches, the tradition of decorating the bride's conveyance continued. In formal weddings the bride would be covered by her veil until it was lifted during the taking of vows, or she would throw it back as she left the church. The wedding veil derived from the flammeum, the saffron-coloured veil used in Roman and Greek times to completely envelop the bride. Yellow was the colour sacred to Hymen, the god of marriage. The veil signified modesty and mystery but did not become an important element of bridal dressing until the 1860s. The origin of the floral head-dress is its symbolic meaning of maidenhood. It was usually made of orange-blossom. White gloves were another emblem of maidenhood.

VISIONS IN WHITE 27

WHEN MAUD AIRINI TIAKITAI DONNELLY married Frank Perry in 1899 it was described as 'the event of this colony'. Maud was the daughter of wealthy land-owning parents in Hawke's Bay. Her mother, the chiefly Ngati Kahungungu 'Princess' Airini (seen to the left of the bride), had inherited vast tracts of land around Hastings, and the Donnellys were prominent social figures who raced horses and went to Government House balls in Wellington. Maud's wedding reflected their status. She wears rich white duchesse satin, the front draped with lace and caught with sprays of orange-blossom. The emblem of the Prince of Wales and the words 'Ich Dien' were embroidered on the train. By the 1890s fashionable grooms were back in frock coats: Frank Perry wears a black double-breasted coat and top hat. There were 600 guests at the wedding and the huge array of gifts were displayed in the drawing-room of the Donnelly residence, Crissoge, on the front porch of which this photograph was taken. The bridal carriage was pulled by four white horses and a banner inscribed with the word 'happiness' hung in the church grounds. The wedding breakfast was served in a white and scarlet marquee by white- and scarlet-clad maids. The best champagne was served and the wedding cake, topped by a Maori canoe rowed by cupids, was six feet high.

CHAPTER TWO

The Grand Occasion
WEDDINGS IN THE EDWARDIAN ERA

WEDDINGS BECAME MAJOR SOCIAL EVENTS in the Edwardian era for people of all social and economic classes. Even daughters of families of quite modest means aspired to a white wedding. To some extent it was a statement by the newly enriched lower middle class that they were as good as anyone else. The 'class' level of wedding frocks is sometimes revealed only by a close inspection of the material, the stitching and the label on the garment. Magazines and newspapers contained long reports of weddings – a practice which survived until the 1970s – and popular postcards commonly featured weddings. This series shows five views from a number of stereoscope photographs produced in about 1900 by R Y Young: 'Dressing the Bride', 'The Fainting Bride', 'The Wedding Ring Guards the Engagement Ring', 'The Wedding Breakfast – The Bride Cuts the Cake', and 'Planning for the Future'.

THE GRAND OCCASION 29

⇌ THESE TWO BRIDES ILLUSTRATE HOW wedding styles evolved in the early years of the century. Victorian stiffness was replaced by filmy fabrics and soft draping. The dress chosen by Cecilia Gallaher of Westport for her marriage to Arthur Hounsell in 1901 is made of a firm fabric and the neckline is high. The white insert in the neckline, called a chemisette, could be removed after the wedding, allowing the dress to be used for future evening occasions. The decorative effect of Mrs Hounsell's outfit is achieved through the use of embroidery and appliqué, as well as the lavishly embroidered veil and flowers. The later photograph of Muriel Boyd shows a softer look and choice of fabric. The frock is made of light lace and tulle, except for the grand satin train. She wears an ornate lace mantilla, her arms are bare and her neckline, although cut low, is covered with a filmy lacy chemisette. The pouched bosom and tiny waist are typical of the Edwardian period. Muriel married George Hoby at Nelson Cathedral in 1907.

THE FAMILIES OF TRADESMEN AND ARTISANS put considerable expense into weddings during the early years of the century, with special wedding clothes, professionally made bouquets and studio photographs. Maggie Battersby was one of six daughters of a drainlayer contractor who lived in Morningside, Auckland. The groom, Sidney Edwin Totman, was a chef. Lace, muslin, pin-tucking and flounces decorated her dress and those of her bridesmaids when she married in Auckland in 1905. The two older bridesmaids, who are her sisters, wear large Edwardian hats. Black stockings were commonly worn during these years, even with delicate frocks. The groom and his groomsmen wear their best lounge suits.

THE WEDDING OF CYRIL WARD to Elinor Davidson at Wellington in 1908 was a high-society event. The bridegroom's father was Sir Joseph Ward, the Prime Minister, and a large contingent of parliamentarians and social leaders attended the event. The day was also celebrated as the silver wedding anniversary of Sir Joseph and Lady Ward. The bride wears silk satin, with a long train and plain veil. Her bridesmaids, Eileen Ward (left) and Gladys Webster, wear similar but not matching dresses and carry fashionable flower-decorated wands. The page-boy is Awarua Patrick Ward, brother of Cyril. Other photographs of this wedding show a huge array of gifts, mostly silver, laid out in the billiard-room.

↠ THE WARETA-TAMUMU WEDDING WAS held in 1912, probably at Wanganui. The bride wears draped silk satin with a long train, lace chemisette, and lace gloves. The youthful bridegroom also wears white gloves, with a white bow-tie. The flower-girls wear velvet dresses and the mob caps popular during this period. The page-boys wear velvet suits with lacy collars. The custom of using small children, especially little boys, in the bridal party had become popular in the late nineteenth century. The boys were often put in historical fancy dress for the occasion.

BY THE TWENTIETH CENTURY THE white wedding was common even among working families, such as the Hawthorne family of Puponga, near Nelson. The men were clearly miners, and the groom wears a working-man's cap rather than a fashionable bowler or top hat.

THE GRAND OCCASION 35

MEMBERS OF THE ROBINSON FAMILY of Collingwood, a mining area near Nelson, celebrate a wedding in 1903. The bride, standing centre, has her best dress on, but does not wear a veil. The bodice and upper sleeves are heavily pin-tucked, she wears an orange-blossom spray and carries Christmas lilies. The seated groom wears his best dark suit, white tie, and white handkerchief in his pocket. The mother of the bride holds a bouquet – it was quite common at the time for the mothers of both the bride and the groom to have flowers. The party has rigged up a tent as backdrop and garlanded it with flowers. They are planning to have a good time, judging by the accordion held by the man at the back. Group photographs in the garden or back yard were quite common for all social classes.

TESLA COLLECTION, ALEXANDER TURNBULL LIBRARY G16851 1/1

THIS SIMPLE WEDDING TABLE WITH flowers from the garden provides a detailed record of the fare at a breakfast for an artisan or tradesman's family. Apart from the decorated wedding cake, most of the food appears homemade. There are sandwiches, pies, scones, slabs of fruit cake and bowls of jelly. Food at a wedding breakfast was usually cold. A large supply of beer waits on the sideboard.

THE WEDDING 'BREAKFAST' WAS so named because until 1886 weddings were held in the morning. In that year, a change in the canonical hours made afternoon weddings possible but the name 'breakfast' stuck. Many homes could not accommodate a large wedding party, and it was not usual to hire a venue. The large tent or marquee enabled a considerable number of people to be entertained. In this Edwardian wedding party, the bride is seated to the left of the cake at the centre table. The bottles of wine and wine glasses signify that this family was one of some means. The flower-decorated marriage bell is a traditional wedding decoration which could be placed in the church or at the reception. If its petals fell on the bride, this was meant to bring good luck.

Marvels of the Confectioners' Art
WEDDING CAKES

THE WEDDING CAKE IS ONE of the oldest wedding customs. Cakes were associated with weddings as far back as Roman times. However, the traditional tiered wedding cake is actually a mid-nineteenth-century invention, popularised by the British. Before then, there was a heavy fruity groom's cake and a lighter decorated bride's cake. The style of the modern wedding cake evolved in stages. Elizabeth Raffald, a confectioner from Manchester, developed the 'plumb cake' as a bride cake and in 1769 first published directions for double icing a cake with marchpane or marzipan and white sugar icing. Piping was invented by a French confectioner in the early 1800s and this led to the heavy encrustation of cakes. It was left to royalty to put the final touches on this creation. Queen Victoria's wedding cake had been a single round cake, three yards in circumference and weighing 300 pounds, but in 1858, the firm of Gunter and Ward in London created the first tiered cake for the wedding of the Princess Royal. This was six or seven feet high, in three tiers, surmounted with cupids. Flowers usually topped the classic cake, at first real flowers in a silver vase, but later artificial flowers in a sugar vase. Cakes were elaborately decorated with 'favours' of ribbons, horseshoes, bells and other good-luck charms. These would be given out to guests. Silk or paper banners inscribed with the initials of the couple could also be hung from the cake. Tiered cakes were difficult to cut and had to be dismantled. The cutting of the cake and distribution of pieces became one of the prime rituals of the wedding breakfast.

↢ AUSTRALIANS ARE CREDITED WITH CHANGING the shape of wedding cakes. In the 1950s Australian housewives enthusiastically embraced the art of sugarcraft and competed at agricultural shows. 'Plastic icing' and sugarpaste enabled elaborate flowers to be modelled. The cakes became more rounded in shape with flat top surfaces. This spectacular cake was made in 1988 by a team led by Dorothy Miles and Doreen Blundell of Sugarcraft New Zealand for the wedding of Masina and Sereti Willy Toleafoa at Auckland. There were 21 separate cakes which took 250 hours to design, bake and decorate. The baking alone took 37 hours and the cake cost $1500. It was Masina's 21st birthday as well as her wedding, and there were 400 guests. The head of each family at the Samoan wedding received one cake.

↢ IN FRANCE AND BELGIUM the giant croquembouche is the traditional wedding cake. The cake is cone shaped, and built up of small round choux pastries filled with confectioner's cream and dipped in hot toffee. Lisa Cacala and Ian Clark chose a croquembouche made by the Regent Hotel for their wedding at Auckland in 1990. Lisa's ivory silk dress was made by Marilyn Sainty.

CHAPTER THREE

Plain Elegance
THE FIRST WORLD WAR PERIOD

TYREE STUDIO COLLECTION, NELSON PROVINCIAL MUSEUM

IMMEDIATELY BEFORE THE FIRST WORLD WAR radical changes began to occur in women's clothing as women entered the workforce in larger numbers than ever before. Comfort and practicality began to influence style. Without tight corseting, the waist became less important and the dress line became less curvaceous and more sheath-like. Mrs Harvey wears a plain but elegant wedding dress, which depends for its effect on cut rather than decoration. The cross-over tunic style gives a Grecian appearance which is emphasised by the classic two-yard-square veil. The dress is bunched at the hem with a large buckle and the hem is decorated with seed pearls. A tabard-like panel falls from the shoulders to form a train.

WEDDINGS ALWAYS BECOME PLAINER IN wartime. Frivolity is deemed to be inappropriate and marriages are brought forward when men are enlisting and being called up. Rhoda Wishaw chose a plain but fashionable travelling suit for her wedding to James Barnard in 1916. As can be seen from her bridesmaid's outfit, hems had started to creep up. After the war, the Barnards farmed near Masterton, initially living in a tent.

PLAIN ELEGANCE 43

F N JONES COLLECTION, ALEXANDER TURNBULL LIBRARY G28952 1/2

ALTHOUGH SOME wartime brides and grooms chose a small, quiet wedding, others did not, and as shown in this photograph taken in Wellington about 1915, some brides continued to wear white. A wide range of men's wartime uniform styles are displayed in this large wedding party. As can be seen from the bridesmaids, white stockings have come back into vogue.

BRIDES IN UNIFORM WERE VERY uncommon before the Second World War. This Salvation Army wedding group, photographed about 1920, has made few concessions to the event. It is even debatable which is the bride. The man with the buttonhole at first glance seems to be the groom, but the woman whose chair he is holding appears not to be wearing a wedding ring, while the woman in the centre of the group is. Her banner reading 'God first' must have sent a clear message to a new husband! This may even have been a double wedding as it was customary for Salvation Army brides to wear a white silk bridal cord or scarf draped from shoulder to hip at their weddings. In a uniformed Salvation Army wedding, the couple face the congregation to take their vows, and the officiating officer joins their hands.

THE BENZIES FAMILY CELEBRATE the wedding of Lieut. William Benzies to Isabella Lawrence of Banffshire, Scotland, under an improvised canvas awning about 1917. The bride, photographed in the act of cutting the cake, wears a high-waisted dress, and a veil low on her forehead. The guests are enjoying cake and tea, poured both from a silver teapot – held by the standing man – and a chipped enamel teapot – seen on the verandah. The Benzies family lived at Benachie, Tasman, Nelson.

PLAIN ELEGANCE 45

A VERY YOUTHFUL MR AND MRS MARSHALL have chosen street clothes for their wedding. She wears a plain costume with vandyke stitching, button trim and pleated, side-buckled satin belt, and carries lily of the valley. The groom and groomsman wear the lounge suits and bowler hats which were starting to become standard wear for many grooms. Although this couple is probably in their late teens or early twenties, the legal marriage age at this time was even lower: twelve for girls and fourteen for boys. This was changed to sixteen for both sexes in 1933 after decades of agitation from women's organisations.

Little Charmers
BRIDESMAIDS AND FLOWER GIRLS

The Moyes bridesmaids, c. 1878.

The Bain bridesmaids, c. 1892.

LITTLE CHARMERS

The Prussing bridesmaids, c. 1905.

The Baltrop girls, c. 1920.

The groom and flower-girl at the Brown-Thompson wedding, 1959.

FLOWERS REPRESENT FERTILITY AND are part of wedding ceremonies in most parts of the world. The flower-girl has her origins in the tradition of strewing flowers in the bride's path. Historically, the bridesmaids' role was to protect the bride from evil spirits, which explains the practice of dressing the bridesmaids in similar costumes to the bride to outwit evil-wishers. This was a perilous role for the bridesmaids, hence the saying: 'Thrice a bridesmaid, never a bride.' Good-luck symbols abound in nuptial practices. Sounding car horns is supposed to scare off evil spirits, as firing guns or ringing bells had in earlier times. The practice of wearing 'something old, something new, something borrowed, something blue' is also aimed at bringing good luck to the bride. A coin sewn into the hem of a frock or slipped into a shoe is thought to bring prosperity and good fortune.

CHAPTER FOUR

The Flapper Brides

WEDDINGS IN THE 1920s

✈ AMY HARPER'S ORIGINAL BRIDAL STUDIO, Glenmore Studios, was in Eden Terrace, Auckland. The tradition of recording weddings in photographs provided steady work for photographic studios from the late nineteenth century, and many studios, such as Glenmore, were able to supply an elegantly decorated wedding car. Wedding photography was highly stylised and conservative. Particular conventions were broken only gradually. Bridal parties received the same standard photographs. Smiling brides or contact between bride and groom were innovations which in most studios did not occur until after the Second World War.

THE FLAPPER BRIDES 49

FOR DECADES WEDDING PORTRAIT STYLES were very formalised with the couple or party squarely facing the camera. Amy Harper, the doyenne of Auckland wedding photographers, broke with tradition by experimenting with more informal styles. Harper liked to arrange her groups to emphasise the relationships between people. In this portrait from 1922 she has faced the party sideways, and the bride, Edith Wadley, has taken Alf Battersby's arm. The convincing backdrop adds to the effect of the party leaving the church. At the beginning of the 1920s, skirts were rising, although only very discreetly.

50 THE FLAPPER BRIDES

THE BRIDE AND GROOM RETREAT INTO the decorated Newport taxi in Nelson to escape flying confetti. The practice of throwing small pieces of cut-up paper has its origins in ancient fertility rituals, where seeds, wheat or rice were showered over the couple to ensure they successfully produced offspring. Strewing the bride with petals has a similar meaning, as has the almond icing on bridal cakes. In recent years confetti has been banned at some churches because of the mess, or areas have been set aside for it to be thrown.

THE FLAPPER BRIDES 51

THE 'RECOGNITION' WEDDING CEREMONIAL developed in the 1920s. As the bride and groom left the church they walked through a guard of honour marking an occupational or interest group. Objects such as swords, tennis rackets, or rowing blades could form an archway for the couple. In keeping with its status as a rite of passage, only the couple and not the wedding party passed through the archway. It appears in this photograph that the bride must have been a member of a gun club.

FLAPPER BRIDES WORE SHORT SKIRTS, filmy fabrics and pale silk stockings: hems lifted steadily through the decade. Ropes of pearls were *de rigueur*. Headwear became quite inventive, but veils were usually made of light, frothy tulle which came low down onto the forehead and was held towards the back of the head. Wedding dresses in the 1920s featured superb cut and exquisite fabrics rather than heavy beading or trimming, to achieve a delicate, rather ethereal effect. Not only were legs exposed but arms were also bared in sleeveless dresses. The modernity of the costume contrasted with its fragility, adding to the aura of vulnerability surrounding the bride. Mrs Ellis wears a sunray veil, and a lace shift over a silk frock. Mrs Roe's scalloped hem and her bridesmaid's vandyke hem were fashionable around 1928. The bridesmaid's tulle bandeau and shingle contribute to a very stylish wedding portrait.

BY THE LATE TWENTIES, a back-dipping hem was fashionable as seen when Myrtle Williams married Thomas Hewitt at Levin in 1929. The bride wears appliquéd and ribbon-embroidered organza with a lace sunray veil. The bride sewed all the head-dresses and outfits herself. The fairy-tale effect of this beautiful bridal party is perhaps explained by Mr and Mrs Hewitt's involvement in the theatre. During the 1920s and 1930s they staged large pantomimes in the Levin area. The men's white gloves, wing collars and white bow-ties are seen in many twenties' wedding portraits.

54 THE FLAPPER BRIDES

IRENE HELLEN MORGAN WORE a simple shift with a very short skirt when she married Stanley Rush, a builder, at Auckland in 1929. She is engulfed in an elaborately embroidered veil. The bridesmaid, her sister Doris Morgan, wore a cloche hat and salmon-pink voile dress. The gold arm bracelet was a gift from the bridegroom. The tradition that the bridegroom should give jewellery, often pearls, to the bridesmaids was observed at weddings for many years.

THE FLAPPER BRIDES 55

→ WHEN 'AUNT GWEN' OF RADIO 2YA's children's programme married Bruce Stennett of Sydney ('Uncle Bruce') in January 1930 it was a huge media event. An estimated 30,000 listeners heard the service in what was billed as 'the first radio wedding'.

'In response to the call of Love itself she needs must leave our shores and bid a fond farewell to Radioland, her unseen multitude of fairy helpers have hallowed the marriage altar with their presence and placed on her bridal finger the gift of gifts.'

As Aunt Gwen, Gwendoline Dagmar Shepherd had listeners up and down New Zealand so interest in her wedding was intense. Around 2000 well-wishers gathered at the St Paul's Pro-Cathedral in Wellington when she married. The bride wears a gown of ivory net and lace over georgette finished with a large bow of shell-pink and white satin on the left side. Her ivory net veil is embroidered in silver and falls from a coronet of pearls. The matron of honour ('Aunt Huia', sister of the bride) and the three bridesmaids all wear deep pink, and carry pink sweet peas.

CHAPTER FIVE

The Glamour Weddings

HOLLYWOOD INFLUENCES THE 1930s

CINEMA, ESPECIALLY THE ROMANTIC historical epics of the period, influenced the wedding dresses of the 1930s. These were svelte, elegant and sophisticated, clinging to the body and sweeping into a long rounded train. Gowns were usually cut on the bias, with minimal decoration, relying on the line and richness of fabric for effect. The fashionable Juliet cap head-dress worn by this unidentified bride creates a neat head shape.

THE GLAMOUR WEDDINGS 57

ROYALTY CONTINUED TO SET WEDDING STYLES. Like many other brides of the time, Jean Auger took her inspiration from the widely reported wedding of the Duke and Duchess of Kent in 1934. Princess Marina wore a clinging silver lamé dress with a cowl neck by Molyneux while a tiara held her long tulle veil. 'Princess Marina' tiaras in diamanté or pearls became a feature of the 1930s. The medieval appearance of Jean Auger's wedding group, with the almost nun-like dresses and abbess-style hats, is typical of the mid-1930s. Jean married John Carline at Auckland about 1935. The style also shows the Hollywood influence of film stars such as Carol Lombard, Norma Shearer and Jean Harlow. As the 1930s went on, icy white became the commonest wedding colour, while cream and ivory waned in popularity.

58 THE GLAMOUR WEDDINGS

THE BRIDE IS ALMOST UPSTAGED by her highly decorative bridesmaids in this unidentified group. Bridesmaids in the 1930s often wore 'garden party' dresses and large floppy hats. Diagonal sheaves of flowers, in this case gladioli, became popular in this decade, having first appeared in the 1920s. Pearls also remained an essential part of the wedding costume. The page-boy is an unusual addition to the party as the fashion for including small boys had all but disappeared by this time. Although the bridesmaids may have been able to wear their dresses again, brides' dresses were increasingly becoming a one-day-only outfit.

※ ANOTHER OUTFIT WITH A MEDIEVAL look, worn by Ivy Twidle who married Bryan Pearce, a builder, at Auckland in the mid-1930s. Ivy chose a satin dress resembling a nun's habit, with a pleated panel in the front and wide pleated sleeves. The bridesmaids wear close-fitting lace, with cowl necks, and delicate organza hats.

60 THE GLAMOUR WEDDINGS

A LONG LINE OF VEILED WOMEN attendants accompany the bridal couple at this Italian wedding in the Island Bay Catholic Church in Wellington in May 1939. Luigi Naoro married Maria Concetta Barnao, daughter of Bartolo Barnao and Giuseppa Pirera of Island Bay. Photographs inside churches were very uncommon until the 1960s.

MORE THAN 4000 SPECTATORS JAMMED the roadway around St Patrick's Cathedral in Auckland in 1938 to catch a glimpse of a unique multiple wedding. Four young brides from the tiny Yugoslav village of Novi Vnodol had travelled to New Zealand to wed men whom they had known only in childhood. The men had emigrated to New Zealand in the mid-1920s. None of them spoke English and they had stuck together over the years while living in public works camps. A joint decision was made that it was time to marry. They proposed by letter and the brides had only one week after their arrival in New Zealand in which to renew their acquaintanceship and get their dresses made for the wedding. The brides wear similar but not matching satin dresses and coronets. The couples are, from left to right: Tereza and Milan Baricevich, Maria and Ivan Sebalja, Pauline and Joe Zanich, and Andrina and Ivan Dobrec. The wedding party consisted of family and friends who had emigrated earlier from Novi Vnodol. The men had spent all their savings bringing the women to New Zealand, so the cost of the wedding was met from monetary wedding gifts and loans.

THE BEST MAN HELPS to bring the contents of the hangi to the wedding feast at the Kuiti wedding at Horowhenua in January 1939.

HELEN KUITI AND HER HUSBAND walk arm in arm from the church to the marquee after their marriage. Helen wears a lace dress with embroidered veil and carries fashionable lilies. The bridesmaids, groomsmen, and Mr and Mrs Kuiti senior – holding hands – follow the party.

SOME MAORI ADOPTED THE WHITE WEDDING in its entirety, while others incorporated Maori elements into the ceremonial. Yet others chose a style that was uniquely Maori. At this wedding at Ratana Pa, Wanganui, in the 1930s, the groom wears a conventional dark suit and bow-tie, but his bride wears a traditional piupiu and cloak and carries a mere. She may have been a member of a Ratana concert party, along with the other women in the group. The woman on the left of the front row wears the outfit of an awhina or sister of the Ratana church and the ministers wear vestments bearing the Ratana insignia, as does the fine woven mat on the floor. The man on the right is T W Ratana, founder of the Ratana movement.

THE GLAMOUR WEDDINGS 65

KINGSFORD STUDIO COLLECTION, NELSON PROVINCIAL MUSEUM

DURING ALL PERIODS SOME BRIDES continued to wear street clothes at their weddings. Mrs Davis wears a plain but beautifully cut crêpe frock with a finely ruched detail at the neck and a wide-brimmed fine straw hat. Mr Davis wears a well cut dark lounge suit. They married in Nelson about 1939.

CHAPTER SIX

Hasty Marriages and Fabric Shortages
WEDDINGS IN THE SECOND WORLD WAR PERIOD

THE 1939 ANNOUNCEMENT THAT NEW ZEALAND was at war provoked a rapid increase in weddings. Marriages were often hastily arranged, brought forward by the imminent departure of men overseas. Many brides married in street clothes just as they had in the First World War. The idea of a lavish wedding didn't sit well with wartime urgency and austerity. Rationing of fabrics and foods such as eggs, sugar and butter also restricted what brides could use to make costumes, cakes and wedding breakfasts. Where wedding dresses were worn, they were often designed to serve later as an evening frock.

HASTY MARRIAGES AND FABRIC SHORTAGES 67

BOTH BRIDE AND GROOM were sometimes in uniform as in this study of a wedding breakfast from 1944. The women are wearing tropical dress, suggesting that the wedding took place at one of the overseas camps staffed by the WAACs during the war.

68 HASTY MARRIAGES AND FABRIC SHORTAGES

✈ WHEN CAPTAIN W L DILLON of Wellington and Sister Eve Rolston of Christchurch married in the mid-1940s it was the first all-Kiwi wedding among the British Commonwealth Occupation Force stationed in Japan. The pair, members of the New Zealand Expeditionary Force, were married at 6 New Zealand General Hospital, and are shown walking to the sisters' mess for the reception between a guard of honour of Japanese house-girls.

HASTY MARRIAGES AND FABRIC SHORTAGES 69

IN BOTH WORLD WARS NEW ZEALAND men brought home brides from countries in which they had fought. In the Second World War, brides also went the other way and 1396 New Zealand women married Americans who had been in New Zealand on leave or recuperating from wounds. More than 600 of the brides belonged to the Auckland YWCA's American Kiwi Club set up to prepare them for life on the other side of the world. Women were divided into 'state' groups in the hope that friendships begun in New Zealand would provide support in the new land.

KINGSFORD STUDIO COLLECTION, NELSON PROVINCIAL MUSEUM

EVEN IN WARTIME THERE WERE SOME glamour weddings. Norman Wilkes and Gwendaline Frank are shown with a suitably decorated Nelson taxi outside the Nelson Cathedral. The bride wears guipure lace and strappy high heels. Most men now wore a dark lounge suit rather than the formal morning coat. Hats were not favoured by men, but a white flower usually adorned the buttonhole and a white handkerchief could be inserted in the breast pocket.

MANY ELEMENTS OF THE POST-WAR wedding are seen in the costumes at the wedding of Norma Best and Leonard Tear held at Nelson in 1951. Norma Best wears a satin brocade gown designed by Miss Sparks Of Christchurch. It has a draped fichu collar over the shoulders and side-draped panniers on the skirt. The dress extends into a long curved train which is overlaid with an equally long bridal veil. Her bridesmaid wears lavender satin with a sweetheart neckline and panniers on the skirt and a tiny matching cap. Bridesmaid and flower girl carry ruched muffs decorated with ribbons and sprigs of violets and lavender. The bride carries a white Bible with winter roses.

The Cresswell-Russell wedding, 1949.

The Kyle-Robinson wedding, 1949.

The Cole-Rose wedding, 1948.

BY THE POST-WAR PERIOD the form of the wedding had become fixed and there was little variation for the next two decades. A number of rituals had to be carried out and each of these would be duly recorded by the photographer hired for the occasion. These included the bride leaving the house, the bride and bridesmaids arriving at the church, the signing of the register, the couple leaving the church, confetti-throwing, and the presentation of a lucky horseshoe to the bride. At the reception the photographer recorded the bride and groom jointly cutting the cake, the best man reading the telegrams, and the couple leaving for the honeymoon. In the 1960s further scenes were added to the photographer's repertoire including scenes inside the church, a shot of the couple in the back seat of the car, the bridegroom kissing the bride and a curious portrait of the bride and groom gazing into a mirror which was revealed when the wedding cake was removed from its stand. Soft satin dresses with sweetheart necklines and long sleeves gathered at the shoulder were the preferred style for brides after the war. Persistent fabric shortages precluded full skirts or sweeping trains. Increasingly the bridal dress was a one-day-only dress which would be difficult to convert to an evening gown.

An unknown wedding about 1949.

The Cole-Rose wedding, 1948.

The Burton-Treacher wedding, 1950.

The Hole-Brown wedding, 1949.

The Nuptial Bounty
WEDDING PRESENTS

F N JONES COLLECTION, NELSON PROVINCIAL MUSEUM

DISPLAYING THE WEDDING GIFTS BECAME a custom during the Victorian period. Presents were exhibited at the wedding reception or at the bride's parents' or the newly married couple's home. Until around the time of the Second World War, the gifts tended to be decorative items which were kept for 'best'. As most middle-class women expected to have at least one servant or some other form of domestic help, kitchenware was never given. Most young women kept a glory box in which they collected their trousseau consisting of more practical items such as blankets and sheets as well as night clothes, table cloths and napkins they stitched themselves. This display from Nelson shows the range of gifts given to a middle-class couple: carving sets, silver cruets, toast racks, spoons, teapots, china jugs, salad bowls, biscuit barrels, serving dishes, clocks and vases. Each gift has a card identifying the giver. Perhaps the most surprising gifts are the five framed pictures for the wall. The gifts were given to James Wickham Brown and Emeline Mary Hannah Jones who married at the All Saints Church, Nelson, in 1906.

A FAR MORE PRACTICAL RANGE of gifts was displayed at the wedding of Eileen Fisher to Peter Swan at Auckland in 1969. Almost all women were now expected to do their own cooking and housework. In a sense the gifts defined the social and domestic role women played. In the post-war period the range of household goods widened, and considerable glamour and modernity was attached to home appliances, stainless-steel items and imported ovenware. The gifts given to the new Mr and Mrs Swan include electric frypan, toaster, iron, hot-water jug, heaters, pressure cooker, stainless-steel roasting dishes, mixing bowls, coffee percolator, pottery casseroles, spice sets, blankets and two sets of kitchen scales.

CHAPTER SEVEN

Conservative Years

LITTLE CHANGE IN THE 1950s

TE AO HOU COLLECTION, NATIONAL ARCHIVES

ALTHOUGH MANY MAORI ADOPTED the white church wedding from an early date, traditional taumau marriages also continued. In these, the couple's families or whanau agreed to the marriage at a meeting or taumau. The taumau might be initiated by the couple or by their elders. This public expression of approval of the union constituted the marriage. Successive marriage laws required Maori to conform to Pakeha legal practices, although before the passage of the Maori Purposes Act in 1951, customary or informal marriage was recognised as legal for some purposes. According to the Act, for a marriage to be legal, there must be a formal ceremony, registration and a marriage certificate. Finally, the 1955 Marriage Act denied legality to unions established according to Maori practice.

PHOTOGRAPHS WERE RARELY TAKEN INSIDE the church before the 1960s. Local photographer Olaf Petersen photographed this low-key wedding at a Roman Catholic church in West Auckland in the 1950s.

AFTER YEARS OF DRESS MATERIAL shortages, brides in the 1950s made extravagant use of fabric. Dior's New Look of the late 1940s, with nipped-in waist and wide skirt, signalled a return to feminine curves. Marilyn Luff wanted a Spanish look for her gown when she married Roger Denton at Nelson in 1958. Her dress is made of flocked hailstone nylon and 72 metres of swiss embroidery edged the flounces. The bride carries water lily buds and flowers with ribbons and maidenhair. Marilyn called this a 'rainbow wedding' as the bridesmaids wore salmon pink, teal blue and pale blue. She arranged the bridal group about which the photographer, Geoffrey Wood, was not initially happy. Later he displayed the photograph in his studio.

CONSERVATIVE YEARS 79

THE 1950s WAS A RELATIVELY CONSERVATIVE period for weddings as little changed during the decade. As prosperity returned after the war, there was a revival of the impressive gown made for the wedding day alone. Heavy satins and brocades were popular, creating a dramatic, formal, sculptured look in wedding dresses. Gowns were not usually decorated or adorned. Sleeves tended to be long and closely fitting and necklines were lower than they had ever been before. Veils became less important and head-dresses were perched on the crown of the head. The bride at the Patterson-Moore wedding held at Nelson in 1958 wears a typically stately and well cut brocade dress, its only decorative feature a large fabric bow on the train. 'Half-hats', wired to grip the head, were popular headwear for bridesmaids in the 1950s.

↦ VERY LARGE TRAINS WERE a feature of many wedding costumes in the 1950s. The sumptuous spread of brocade in Mrs B Fraser's dress has proven irresistible for Goldie the cat.

↦ ANOTHER LARGE TRAIN, THIS TIME in the same lace as the dress. Betty Abercrombie was the epitome of the early fifties bride when she married John Wymer at St David's Church in Khyber Pass, Auckland, in 1952.

↦ WHEN GWEN WONG-TOI MARRIED Albert Ernest Sai Louie in 1952 it was an alliance of two long-established New Zealand Chinese families. Gwen wears white satin silk; her bridesmaids pale pink. Gwen's sister (left) and brother (third from right) were attendants and other relatives formed the rest of the bridal party. The wedding took place at the St Luke's Presbyterian Church at Remuera, Auckland. Many New Zealand Chinese were devout Christians and followed Christian wedding practices. In Auckland, a Chinese Presbyterian Church was founded in Cook Street, and women in the congregation, including Gwen Sai Louie, formed a women's fellowship in 1955.

An Abundance of Flowers
BRIDAL BOUQUETS OVER THE YEARS

ALICE ELLEN LILIUM STIDOLPH CARRIED a fine example of a Victorian posy when she married Christian Peter Berg at her parents' home in Wellington in August 1898. Daisies and lily of the valley are held in a paper doily set around a cardboard holder, and white ribbons fall from the arrangement. Particular flowers were traditionally associated with weddings, especially roses, lily of the valley, madonna lilies, arum lilies, orange blossom, myrtle, marigolds, rosemary and gypsophila. Most of these flowers have associations with virginity or fertility. A bride's floral wreath, worn on her hair, symbolised maidenhood, and its removal the end of maidenhood. Mrs Berg's orange-blossom wreath was probably made of wax, or silk padded with cotton wool. This was meant to be destroyed within a month of the wedding to prevent good luck turning to ill. The bridegroom's buttonhole was called a boutonnière.

AN ABUNDANCE OF FLOWERS 83

EDWARDIAN BRIDES FAVOURED LARGE trailing shower bouquets which could reach the hem of the women's frocks. The flowers were wired to hold them among the cloud of maidenhair, asparagus and silver ferns. Roses, daisies and dahlias were the main flowers used in the bouquets for the Potter wedding in 1911. The vast hats are good examples of their period. A bridegroom traditionally paid for the wedding bouquets as well as flowers for his own and the bride's mother.

84 AN ABUNDANCE OF FLOWERS

HUGE, FULL-BLOWN, OLD-FASHIONED ROSES with asparagus fern and maidenhair create a sumptuous bouquet to enrich the simplicity of Bella Battersby's pearl-trimmed muslin frock. The veil has moved low over the forehead compared with Victorian and Edwardian styles, although it would move even further forward as can be seen in the next photograph. Bella, a tailoress, married George Kenny, a salesman, at Auckland in 1921.

CASUAL SHEAVES OF FLOWERS which were nursed like a baby became popular in the 1920s and 1930s. At this double wedding held in January 1921, the brides carry irises simply tied with a ribbon, and the four bridesmaids cradle bundles of long-stalked flowers. The wedding party is carefully co-ordinated: all the men wear spats on their shoes and the brides' attendants wear tulle sunflower hats.

AN ABUNDANCE OF FLOWERS 85

FORMAL ARRANGEMENTS OF ARUM LILIES were in vogue during the 1930s. Their sculptural effect matched the sinuous line of the bias-cut wedding gowns of the period. Traditionally, the bridal bouquet was thrown in the air before the bride went upstairs to change, the lucky person who caught it being expected to marry next.

FROM THE 1950s TO THE 1970s brides often chose tiny arrangements of flowers, and in some cases artificial elements such as ribbons almost overwhelmed the blooms. In the 1970s a single rose or two carnations were all that some brides carried. Swiss-born Dolores Sunier chose a simple two-orchid and maidenhair spray for her wedding to Neville Dimock at Nelson in 1957. She wears a white satin ballerina-length, princess-line frock with a boat neckline and pearl details. The short veil is held by a Tudor-style satin and pearl head-dress.

IN THE 1980s AND 1990s bridal bouquets came in a wide range of styles, from Victorian posies to the cascade bouquet chosen by Barbara Stein for her wedding to David Raos in Auckland in 1991. The bouquet is made entirely of peach-coloured roses to match her silk duchesse satin dress with beaded chantilly lace bodice made by Rosemary Smith. Barbara's head-dress is made of eighteen matched real roses.

CHAPTER EIGHT

Changing Traditions
WEDDINGS IN THE 1960s AND 1970s

➤ THE BEST MAN AMUSES the wedding guests at the wedding of Mr and Mrs Vercoe held at Waikanae in the mid-1960s. It was customary for the bride to remain silent while speeches were made by the groom, the best man and her father. By the 1990s brides and bridesmaids were quite likely to make their own speeches.

CHANGING TRADITIONS 87

THE PRIEST BLESSES THE BRIDE AND GROOM at this wedding held at Torere in 1963. The bride wears plain satin with a bell-shaped skirt and an embroidered veil held by a satin circlet.

THE INCREASINGLY DIVERSE RANGE of cultural groups in New Zealand was reflected in unique wedding styles. More than 500 people packed the Pukekohe War Memorial Hall to celebrate a double wedding of two brothers who wed two sisters in December 1960. Sarjit Kore married Sakattar Singh Birak and Pritam Kore married Ganges Singh Birak. In this Sikh wedding, the couples, garlanded with flowers, are shown sitting in front of a decorated canopy called the mandil. The men wear European suits, the women saris.

EILEEN FISHER WORE A STRAIGHT CHAMPAGNE-coloured silk velvet sheath at her wedding to Peter Swan at Auckland in 1969. Eileen's dress was inspired by Zeffirelli's *Romeo and Juliet* which was showing in Auckland at the time. Copying costume styles from historical periods was popular in the 1960s. Eileen has a four-tier ivory silk tulle veil held by a matching velvet band. She carries carnations and chrysanthemums in autumn shades. A long train falls from the shoulders. Because her father was dead, Eileen's fifteen-year-old brother, Richard, gave her away.

MERILYN LEXIE WIREN WORE a princess-line satin gown when she married Christopher Savill at the Nelson Cathedral in 1965. Although brides in the 1960s wore a wide range of styles, from short and frilly to long and formal, Merilyn's dress displays many of the hallmarks of the classic sixties dress. The 'backward pull' shape of the outfit, with the court train flowing from the shoulders, was a development of the grand skirts of the 1950s. The favoured line was (viewed from the side) like a right-angled triangle with the train forming the longest edge. The triangular shape is echoed in the tight floral arrangement. Dresses in the 1960s were often high-waisted in an Empire style, with a flat front and minimum of seams. The short, full, bouffant veil is also typical of the period.

KINGSFORD STUDIO COLLECTION, NELSON PROVINCIAL MUSEUM

OLAF PETERSEN PHOTOGRAPH, AUCKLAND INSTITUTE AND MUSEUM

BRIDES IN THE LATE 1960s began to adopt a romantic nostalgic style in frocks. A covered-up 'little-girl' look was popular, with high neck, long cuffed sleeves and lace. Brides in the late sixties and early seventies were generally younger than in earlier times: 21 was the average age for brides in 1971. By contrast, in 1923 brides had been around 26. The average age of grooms had also fallen from 29 to 24 in the same period. The flower, symbol of the decade, was extensively used in costumes and was even woven into fabrics as in the lace dress chosen by this unidentified bride. But there is hardly anything 'little-girl' about the crochet mini-dress with cut-outs that her bridesmaid wears. Olaf Petersen, the photographer who recorded this wedding, called it the 'Sand hills wedding' and the west coast of Auckland can be seen as the backdrop to this scene. Another photograph shows the same bride on horseback. Couples in this period were beginning to challenge fixed conventions around the location and form of the wedding ceremony, a trend which intensified in the 1980s and 1990s. Many weddings were low-key, informal affairs, followed by exuberant partying.

Photographers were also experimenting with new portrait styles. By the 1990s, the seaside wedding photograph had become a cliché; in the 1960s it was highly innovative.

CHANGING TRADITIONS 91

THE 1970s WERE A TIME of breaking with the customs and conventions of the past and weddings did not escape the challenge. This caftan wedding from 1973 shows a definite Eastern influence. The groom, Mr A Brown, and his attendants wear gold-embroidered caftans. Margaret Croskery, the bride, wears Indian muslin and the bridesmaids crimson muslin gowns. All the women carry two carnations. Wedding parties in this decade, while breaking the rules, still usually retained many traditional elements. Mr and Mrs Brown married at St John's Anglican Church at Royal Oak, Auckland, and the bride carries a traditional lucky horseshoe.

WEDDINGS IN THE 1960s AND 1970s displayed a wider range of wedding fashions than any era before or since. Even grooms were adventurous in their dress. At his wedding in 1969 dress designer Perrin McLeod wears a double-breasted black silk suit from Carnaby Street with a floppy silk tie. Breaking with the tradition that the groom should not see his bride's dress until she arrived at the altar, Perrin designed the costume for his wife: a detachable three-tiered ivory wool crêpe cape with piped satin edges worn over a matching dress with tiered sleeves. Sally Hollis, a model, wears a curly brown wig over her own blonde hair which she said didn't harmonise with the poetic effect of the costume. The pair married at All Saints Church, Kilburnie, Wellington.

CHAPTER THIRTEEN

The New Romantics
THE REVIVAL OF THE WHITE WEDDING

SUE GEE PHOTOGRAPH

THE WEDDING OF LADY DIANA SPENCER to the Prince of Wales in 1981 generated a new enthusiasm for romantic fairy-tale weddings and brought to a decisive end the erosion of the traditional white wedding which had been occurring during the seventies. The wedding was broadcast around the world, allowing millions to see Diana's extravagantly frothy cream silk taffeta frock. Following the royal lead, brides chose billowing dress styles, emphasising fullness, lightness and movement. The modern wedding encapsulated romance, glamour and a fine sense of theatre. The imagination was allowed full rein in the creation of the perfect day. Heather Gardner's white dupion silk dress by Rosemary Smith took twelve metres of fabric. The style is classical and romantic with a high curved collar reminiscent of the Norman Hartnell gown Princess Margaret wore at her wedding in 1960. The surprising element is the plunging neckline. Heather married Glen Hitchcock at Auckland in 1987.

THE NEW ROMANTICS 93

SUE GEE PHOTOGRAPH

THE BRIDE AND GROOM ARE HOISTED aloft on chairs at an exuberant Orthodox Jewish wedding. Jewish weddings are very joyous and energetic. Men link arms with men and women join with women to dance in circles. Another custom is to tie serviettes together to form a skipping rope. At this wedding, the bride skipped the rope and was then joined by other women. The actual service takes place with the bride and groom standing under a chuppah or canopy. Some believe this represents the joint home of the couple, others that it symbolises the vast sky under which they are joined. During the ceremony the bride walks several times around her husband. Blessings are made while wine is drunk from a shared cup by the bride, groom and parents, and the groom breaks a wineglass under his foot. This symbolises the destruction of the temple but also the concept that although the wineglass will never be together again, it will not be apart. The wedding of Jacqueline Klisser and Kerry Knight took place in the Jewish Synagogue at Auckland in 1989, with the service conducted primarily in Hebrew. Jacqueline wears a soft pink silk dress by Adrienne Winkelmann with chantilly lace on the hem and sleeves. The groom wears a white festival skull-cap called a kappel.

MANY BRIDAL FROCKS OF THE 1980s and 1990s had a nostalgic retro look, borrowing design elements from previous eras but using them with little regard for historical authenticity. Leg o' mutton sleeves were fashionable in the 1890s but they were never combined with a gathered skirt or low neckline as they are in this bridal competition held in Nelson in 1987. Displaying the shoulders and bosom was a startling departure, signalling a new desire to look alluring and sexy, rather than chaste. Bride of the Year contests, such as this one won by Tania Smith, were held to raise funds for charitable organisations.

NEW ZEALAND HERALD

NOVEL LOCATIONS HAVE BECOME POPULAR as couples strive for a wedding that is 'different'. Maryanne Ranstead wears white with a tiara holding a billowing veil, and the groom, Gary Palmer, wears tails and top hat at this wedding in 1988, but convention ended there. The couple wanted something 'unique' so chose to be the first people married on a jet boat at the base of the Huka Falls near Taupo. Their vows were repeated on land so they could be shared by family and friends. This was also a legal requirement. Until 1994 marriages had to be held 'with open doors' so that the public had access. The removal of these words from the Marriage Act meant that a marriage could be held anywhere as long as it was solemnised by an authorised celebrant, in front of two witnesses. Before this change in legislation, when marriages were celebrated on the water the vessel had to be tied up with the gangplank down. The change also meant that marriages could be celebrated in the air: one couple married in a helicopter hovering over Wellington.

RICHELLE KAHUI JOINS THE DANCE at her wedding to Kelly McConnell which was held at Cheltenham Beach, Auckland, in 1993. Richelle's German Samoan family had gathered from all around the world for the event, and organised the entertainment. The dances were choreographed by Richelle's aunt from Hawaii. Richelle wears a silk dress made by a friend in Sydney to a design she had seen while visiting Europe. The crest of the Stowers family – the maiden name of her mother Nina Makoare – was embroidered on the front of the gown, a task which took seventy-two hours.

THE NEW ROMANTICS 97

KRZYSZTOF PFEIFFER PHOTOGRAPH, AUCKLAND MUSEUM

JULIANA SUCU WORE A UNIQUE BARKCLOTH wedding dress when she married Graeme Couper in a Seventh Day Adventist ceremony in the grounds of Orewa House in 1992. The dress was made by her mother, Mereia Johnston, in a style Juliana chose from a magazine photograph. Mereia learnt the craft of tapa making in her home country of Fiji and brought the art with her when she came to New Zealand with her husband in 1976. The white cloth (masi vulavula) used in the shawl and train was from Somosomo on Taveuni, and the cloth in the dress itself from Vatulele. The shawl was treated with perfumed coconut oil in which flowers had been soaked to make the cloth translucent and take on a golden glow. The train is folded over an attached band at the waist so that a shorter length hangs above the train like a bustle. No veil is worn.

AS ANITA CHAN AND BRENDON HING met and conducted their courting while pursuing their interest in basketball, they mocked up a game for their wedding photographs in 1992. Modern wedding photographers need to be considerably more inventive than their counterparts of forty years ago, who were able to rely on a number of set poses. The traditional dupion silk dress with Alençon lace was designed by Rosemary Smith.

THE NEW ROMANTICS 99

COUPLES WHO DID NOT WANT a church wedding had increasing options in the 1980s and 1990s. A change in legislation in 1977 allowed the use of approved civil marriage celebrants as well as ministers of the church and marriage registrars. A list of approved celebrants is published in the *New Zealand Gazette* every year. Auckland journalist Yvonne van Dongen and barrister James Holland were married by celebrant Winsome Rouse among the autumn leaves of Cornwall Park in 1989. Yvonne wears a white silk Rosaria Hall suit over a lace camisole, with pearls.

100 THE NEW ROMANTICS

GIL HANLY PHOTOGRAPH

✈ WHEN MARYANNE GARDINER AND ALAN MUMMERY married in 1993 they chose to have fun, as it was the second marriage for both of them. The vows were serious, but the ceremony reflected Maryanne's involvement in arts and the theatre. The silver space-suit costumes were hired, and the wedding took place at a favourite Ponsonby café. Guests were asked to bring a bottle of wine for the cellar rather than a present. The couple have continued to 'marry' again each year on their anniversary, and every time in silver space-suits. Maryanne says she wants her daughter Olivia to be able to say that her mother married twenty-five times!

THERE WERE TWO BRIDES AT the wedding of Carmel Carroll, opera singer, and Jess Denholm, gardener, in Auckland in April 1995. The two women arrived at the ceremony together, and, in acknowledgment of Jess's Scottish heritage, were piped into the service together. The couple planned their own ceremony and wrote the vows they exchanged. These were inscribed on a scroll and witnessed by all their friends present. Each woman gave herself to the other. Carmel wears the silk and cotton brocade concert gown with a train she had worn at a New Zealanders at the Aotea Centre Concert. Jess wears Scottish national dress with a black watch tartan kilt. Although the Human Rights Act 1993 outlawed discrimination on the grounds of sexual preference, this did not override the marriage laws. Consequently, while lesbian marriages are legal in the Netherlands and some states of America, they are not yet legal in New Zealand. Having decided they wanted to be together for ever, Carmel and Jess wanted to marry to give status to their relationship so that others would regard their relationship as seriously as they did.

Bibliography

Arch, Nigel, and Marschner, Joanna
The Royal Wedding Dresses
Sidgwick & Jackson, London, 1990

Baker, Margaret
Wedding Customs and Folklore
Rowan and Littlefield, USA, 1977

Barker, Diane
'The confetti ritual'
New Society 1972; 20: 614-17

Boland, Mary Jane
'Wondrous weddings'
New Zealand Herald 22 February 1994

Charsley, Simon L
Wedding Cakes and Cultural History
Routledge, London, 1992

Coney, Sandra
Every Girl: A Social History of Women and the YWCA in Auckland
Auckland YWCA, Auckland, 1986

Coney, Sandra
Standing in the Sunshine: A History of New Zealand Women Since They Won the Vote
Viking, Auckland, 1993

Clark, Rowena
Hatches Matches and Dispatches: Christening, Bridal and Mourning Fashions
National Gallery of Victoria, Australia, 1987

Currie, Dawn H
'"Here comes the bride": The making of a "Modern traditional" wedding in Western Culture'
Journal of Comparative Family Studies 1993; 24: 403-21

Eldred-Grigg, Stevan
Pleasures of the Flesh: Sex and Drugs in Colonial New Zealand 1840-1915
Reed, Auckland, 1984

Ginsburg, Madeline
Wedding Dress 1740-1970
Victoria and Albert Museum/Her Majesty's Stationery Office, London, 1981

Gregg, Stacy
'Wedding belles'
Sunday Star-Times 16 April 1995: D1-2

Horrocks, Eleanor
'Wedding Rituals in Auckland',
Thesis for MA in Anthropology, Auckland University, 1973

Lansdell, Avril
Wedding Fashions 1860-1980
Shire Publications, Aylesbury, 1986

Laverack, Elizabeth
With This Ring: 100 Years of Marriage
Elm Tree Books, London, 1979

Lovell-Smith, Margaret
The Woman Question: Writings by the Women Who Won the Vote
New Women's Press, Auckland, 1992

Macdonald, Charlotte
A Woman of Good Character: Single Women as Immigrant Settlers in Nineteenth-century New Zealand
Allen & Unwin/Historical Branch, Department of Internal Affairs, Wellington, 1990

Makareti
The Old-Time Maori
New Women's Press, Auckland 1986

Olssen, Erik and Levesque, Andree
'Towards a history of the European family in New Zealand' in Peggy Koopman-Boyden (ed) *Families in New Zealand Society*
Methuen, Wellington, 1978

Probert, Christina
Brides in Vogue Since 1910
Thames & Hudson, UK, 1984

Statistics New Zealand
All About Women in New Zealand
Statistics New Zealand, Wellington, 1993

Statistics New Zealand
New Zealand Now: Families
Statistics New Zealand, Wellington, 1994

Swain, Pauline
'Marriage New Zealand-style'
The Listener 8 November 1971: 7

Wood, Val
War Brides
Random Century, Auckland, 1991

Acknowledgements

A number of people and institutions are owed thanks for help in the production of this book. Special mention needs to go to Maurice Watson and other staff at the Nelson Provincial Museum, Joan McCracken at the Alexander Turnbull Library, Eymard Bradley and Eva Yokum at the Museum of New Zealand / Te Papa Tongarewa, Johanne Buchanan of the *New Zealand Herald*, Gordon Maitland at the Auckland Institute and Museum, and Sue Gee, photographer of Auckland.

Many individuals lent family photographs, or allowed their own weddings to be included in the books. Thanks is owed to them. Sue Gee and Rosemary Smith, wedding gown designer, provided insights into modern weddings, as did Lesley Walker of *Bride and Groom* magazine, and Mary Hancock, marriage celebrant.

For weddings occurring within the past 50 years, every effort was made to gain permission from the subjects of photographs where these photographs had been taken by studio photographers whose work is now in public collections. However, this was not always possible. Sometimes the subjects were unidentified, or it proved impossible to trace them because of the lapse of time since the photographs were taken. If people do recognise themselves in photographs, we hope they enjoy their inclusion. They could also contact the museums holding their photographs as they are always pleased to be given identifying details about photographs in their collections.

Index

American Kiwi Club   69

Best man, role of   62, 72, 86

Bride of the Year contests   94

Bridesmaids, role of   12, 46, 47, 54, 86

Chinese weddings   12, 81, 98

Confectioners   9, 38, 39

Confetti   10, 50, 72

Costume*
- bride's   7, 9, 10, 12, 28, 30, 40, 52, 56-58, 66, 72, 78-80, 89-91, 92, 94, 97
- groom's   7, 10, 14, 21, 27, 45, 53, 70, 91
- non-white   15-17, 21, 65, 66
- white   7, 8, 10, 12, 14, 16, 18, 28, 34, 57, 64, 92

Fijian wedding   97

Flowers   20, 21, 23, 26, 31, 35, 37, 38, 47, 50, 58, 82-85

Flower-girls   46, 47

Human Rights Act   101

Immigrants   6, 12

Indian wedding   87

Italian wedding   60

Jewish wedding   93

Lesbian wedding   101

Maori weddings   7, 8, 16, 27, 33, 62-64, 76, 86, 87
- customary marriage   8, 76
- traditional rituals   8

Marriage
- age at   10, 11, 45, 90
- celebrant   12, 95, 99
- de facto   11
- law   8, 45, 76, 95, 99, 101
- rates   6, 10, 11
- reasons for   6, 8, 12, 15
- remarriage   11, 12, 100

Pacific Islands weddings**   12

Page-boys   33, 58

Photography   9, 15, 18, 22, 23, 25, 31, 35, 48, 49, 60, 77, 78, 90, 98

Ratana church   64

Reform dress wedding   24

Rite of passage   6, 51

Royal family, British   7, 9, 11, 14, 38, 57, 92

Salvation Army   43

Samoan weddings   11, 39, 96,

Transport   7, 26, 27, 48, 70, 73

Trousseau   74

Weddings
- breakfast   12, 27, 36, 37, 44, 62, 66, 67
- cakes   10, 27, 36, 38, 39, 44, 50, 66, 72
- church   8, 16, 25, 99
- cost of   6, 61
- customs   6, 8, 10, 12, 18, 38, 47, 51, 72, 85, 91
- dress, see costume
- gifts   27, 32, 74, 75
- location of   12, 90, 95, 99
- ring   10, 12, 43
- rituals, see weddings, customs
- traditional   6, 11, 12, 92
- veil   21, 24, 26, 30, 52, 57, 71, 79, 89
- wartime   9, 41, 43, 66-68

Women - changing role of   6, 8, 10, 11

Yugoslav weddings   61

YWCA   69

*entries relate to general comments on costume rather than descriptions of particular outfits
 see also Reform dress wedding
**see also Samoan weddings and Fijian wedding